SHROPSHIRE

A portrait in colour

BILL MEADOWS & SHIRLEY TART

COUNTRYSIDE BOOKS

Other counties in this series include:

BUCKINGHAMSHIRE LANCASHIRE
CHESHIRE LINCOLNSHIRE
DERBYSHIRE SUFFOLK
DEVON SURREY
ESSEX SUSSEX
LEICESTERSHIRE & RUTLAND WARWICKSHIRE

First published 2001
© Photographs, Bill Meadows 2001
© Text, Shirley Tart 2001

COUNTRYSIDE BOOKS
3 CATHERINE ROAD
NEWBURY, BERKSHIRE

To view our complete range of books,
please visit us at
www.countrysidebooks.co.uk

ISBN 1 85306 690 7

The photograph on page 1 shows a sculpture at Oswestry
entitled 'The Borderland Farmer' and that on page 4
shows a cottage at Worfield

Designed by Mon Mohan
Produced through MRM Associates Ltd., Reading
Printed in Italy

Contents

INTRODUCTION

'A church, a farm — a curling lane
That seeks to find a tail not there
These are the homes of Shropshire men:
When all have passed, this will remain.'

Peter Phillips, *Ode to Shropshire.*

Shropshire, once our biggest inland county, is a wonderful mix of hills and plains, valleys and meadows. A tapestry of ancient history and modern technology, where the remains of an important 1st-century Roman city and a soaring 21st-century town are a few miles and nearly 2,000 years apart. The South Shropshire Hills, the rolling northern plains, the market towns where yesteryear lives on, are part of our heritage and our today, and are perfectly captured here by Bill Meadows' timeless photographs.

At White Church, which became Whitchurch, tight on the border with Cheshire, the composer of the splendid *Merrie England*, Sir Edward German, was born in a pub. And Shropshire's own lakeland, Ellesmere, is a testament to charm on this northern edge of the county. In the west of this loveliest of shires, tucked in a river's embrace, historic Shrewsbury surely remains a gem among our county towns with its timber buildings, cobbled streets and tribute to its famous son, Charles Darwin. By contrast, in eastern Shropshire, the late 20th-century new town of Telford rose from the desolation of the area's industrial past. While going south is truly a journey into an unbeatable pastoral and hillside panorama with villages and hamlets that have changed little over the years.

To our great literary lady Mary Webb, her shire county was not just the centre but the whole of her world, it gave her life its very spark. And with overwhelmingly lovely writing in novels like *Golden Arrow*, *Gone to Earth*, and *Precious Bane*, she well repaid that compliment.

Of Shropshire, Mary Webb said: 'It is a county where the dignity and beauty of ancient things linger long and I have been fortunate … in being born and brought up in its magical atmosphere'.

More than a century on, so have I. Welcome to our homeland.

Shirley Tart

Whitchurch

*'I watched the blackbirds gather and rise in patterned flight and enjoyed thinking that it must
have been their ancestors Caldecott had watched, remembered and used in his picture books.'*
Elizabeth T. Billington on the time spent in Whitchurch by 19th-century illustrator Randolph Caldecott.

Once you know, it makes sense. The name of the north Shropshire town just minutes from the county's border with Cheshire and one of the oldest inhabited towns in the country, simply means 'white church'. As it happens, 18th-century St Alkmund's church is anything but white. A solid, handsome building, it is a rich and burnished sandstone but here's a clue — the church formerly on that site was of white limestone.

St Alkmund's monument to Sir John Talbot, first Earl of Shrewsbury, is a reminder of a great name which survives in more mundane ways to this day. It is given to the Sir John Talbot's Higher School and is well recognised by Salopians everywhere.

Yet Talbot is just one of an illustrious band of names the Whitchurch area can boast. Like composer Sir Edward German who was born in a local pub, in 1862, as plain E. G. Jones. Or like bank clerk Randolph Caldecott (1846–1886) who so beautifully illustrated children's nursery rhyme books and used Brook House Farm at nearby Hanmer as a model for the illustrations of *The House That Jack Built.*

Many buildings, some fine black and white specimens, and artefacts in the old market town (*opposite*) have survived the years admirably. The firm of J. B. Joyce was established in 1690 and still makes impressive tower clocks, found in many of the world's magnificent buildings. If Whitchurch, sprawling on the edge of the sweeping North Shropshire Plain, is relatively unknown to tourists, that's because a busy bypass system diverts most of them neatly round the town en route for Chester, North Wales and beyond.

The town is also home to a famous Cheshire cheese industry and nearby are internationally known moss and peat lands. While set amidst the surrounding farming country are lovely secrets like Oss Mere (*inset*), one of many miniature water features.

Ellesmere

'The only international language is a child's cry.'
Ellesmere's Eglantyne Jebb, founder of the Save the Children Fund.

Not for nothing is the market town of Ellesmere, just three miles from the Welsh border, known as Shropshire's Lakeland. The town itself is quiet and dreamy … and it is the prettiest ride to get there, wherever you start from. Once there, Tudor, Georgian and Victorian buildings tumble in profusion on medieval streets. And all just the shortest walk from the pride of the town — the Mere itself.

Largest of the six glacial meres around this jewel in North Shropshire's crown, it gets the capital letter to its name! An all year round attraction for visitors and locals alike whether you are a bird watcher, a splasher, a walker or just enjoy the waterfront. The Mere covers 116 acres, is more than 60 feet deep and the most accessible of all the meres, amongst which is White Mere shown opposite. The meres were created during the last Ice Age when the glaciers fell away and left clay-lined hollows which became basins for the melted water. The lakeside visitor centre sets you right for the whole area and from that point there is a delightful half-mile waterfront promenade through the Cremorne Gardens. If you're into yet more serious water, there's always the Llangollen Canal, part of the network of canals accessible from Shropshire.

Of lasting importance for humanity, Eglantyne Jebb who founded the Save the Children Fund was born here in 1876.

Today, antiques and gift shops are worth exploring. So is St Mary's church which overlooks the Mere (*inset*) and has a splendid tower built by the Knights of St John. Once inside, historic and architectural features include a 15th-century carved chapel roof.

Ellesmere was once strategically important when the battle lines with Wales were being drawn. On its highest ground, all is still and peaceful today but a Norman castle once stood there to protect the area from Welsh forces.

All these centuries on, Ellesmere is a gem.

Market Drayton

'And gingerbread junks as big as my foot, we ate and we ate and we ate and we ate.'

The local Market Drayton paper, 1884.

It is a jolly reputation to have. A busy town in a rural heartland, Market Drayton's international symbol is gingerbread men (*inset*). Gingerbread has been baked in the town for more than 200 years and in more recent times, the great public relations machine has been at work to promote the Gingerbread Man far and wide.

How did ginger come to Drayton in the first place? All on account of one of Shropshire's greatest sons, Clive of India. He was born in 1725 at Styche Hall, went to school in Market Drayton itself and was a right tearaway by all accounts. But Clive was forgiven when, with distinguished service in India, he won the battles that were to keep the sub-continent under British rule for 200 years. And he brought so much ginger back to Market Drayton that they had to do something with it; gingerbread seemed the obvious answer. Clive is buried in the nearby village of Moreton Say in an unmarked grave, the usual fate of those who killed themselves — he is believed to have cut his own throat.

But many years before that, there was a town on the site. Indeed, a street market has been held in the town every Wednesday since 1245. And believe it or not, they are still marketeering today. Perhaps some produce would have been very different more than 750 years ago when the market was started by the Abbot of Combermere, but food from local growers and fine cheeses remain attractions. Now, fabrics and china from the Potteries just a few miles farther north into Staffordshire, are also much sought after.

Market Drayton also has a children's Wild Animal Trail offering an entertaining exploration of the town and its history by following pawprints to solve nine riddles and track down the wild animals in the heart of the town.

Gingerbread, India's tragic Clive and animal magic. Who could ask for more?

Oswestry

'Like croziers are the curled shoots growing to bless me as I pass.'
A young Wilfred Owen on a local walk with his cousin, Leslie Gunston,
who was later to use the metaphor in one of his own poems.

If Market Drayton's market tradition began in the 13th century, Oswestry's is even older. The town's weekly and bustling market dates back to 1190 with more than 100 stalls still packing the streets today. Largely unspoiled by progress, Oswestry's individual character has been robustly fashioned by the centuries. Streets with names which owe their origins very much to their past — English Walls, Welsh Walls, The Horsemarket, for instance — are linked by ancient, narrow passageways. Hostelries give further clues to Oswestry's importance as a stagecoach and railway town.

The Oswestry and District Agricultural Show (*opposite*) is held each August and draws thousands of visitors. Agriculture and horticulture are enjoyed alongside a fun fair, crafts and many other aspects of rural life.

Its first school was founded in 1407 and is now a Heritage Centre which holds regular exhibitions of local arts and crafts.

The First World War poet Wilfrid Owen was born in the town in 1893 and lived there for four years before moving to Birkenhead. He and his family were later to return to Shropshire, this time to the county town of Shrewsbury. The brooding poet's work caught for eternity the true horror of the Great World War. He was killed in action on the Western Front a week before Armistice was declared in 1918. Owen is treasured by a proud county as one of its own.

Modern Oswestry has the usual shops and stores — 250 of them — and the amenities enjoyed by many 21st-century towns. But back in 1400, Owain Glyndwr laid siege to this Welsh border town, while later, in the Civil War, Oswestry swore allegiance to King Charles before being captured by Cromwell's Roundheads. It was Oliver Cromwell himself who ordered the demolition of the castle, town walls and fortifications. Now, all that remains is the old hill fort (*inset*). And the stirring tales of history.

Wem and Moreton Corbet Castle

*'The women of Wem and a few musketeers
Beat the Lord Capel and all his Cavaliers.'*

Local taunt after a Royalist Civil War attack ended in defeat.

Once a Saxon settlement and now at the heart of the north Shropshire network of delightful market towns and rolling plains, today's Wem (*opposite*) has a floral reputation. It's the home of the modern sweet pea, developed by 19th-century nurseryman Henry Eckford. And every year Wem bursts into summer colour with the Eckford Sweet Pea Show and annual carnival, drawing enthusiasts from all over the country and the world.

Yet there is mystery in this quiet, sunny little town. In 1995, the 90-year-old Town Hall was gutted by fire. A local man took a photograph and when the film was developed, it clearly showed a young girl at the top of the fire escape. She did not appear on any other pictures. Many believe it was the ghost of a young woman whose lighted candle caused a fire in 1677, destroying the town's old timber houses.

Wem has a colourful history. It was almost demolished in a Wars of the Roses battle in the 15th century, and during the Civil War, 200 years later, was attacked by around 5,000 Royalists led by Lord Capel. Parliamentary supporters were helped in their defence by valiant local women.

The town also has a delicious secret — legendary Treacle Mines which the visitor just might discover with the help of a town trail leaflet!

From Wem to Moreton Corbet is a short drive and if you're looking for ruins, this is where you'll find some of the best. The site of a 13th-century Norman castle and tower, it was later joined by a Tudor mansion (*inset*) built in the French style by the Corbet family, which was captured and burned during the Civil War under attack from Parliamentary troops. Curiously, the remains look more as though they were neatly ruined using a set square rather than by the random demolition of battle. The keep and curtain walls are of particular interest.

Hawkstone Park and Hodnet Hall

'The splendour falls on castle walls
And snowy summits old in story:
The long light shakes across the lakes,
And the wild cataract leaps in glory.'
Alfred Lord Tennyson, *The Revenge.*

Mention Hawkstone Park (*opposite*) to locals and you'll immediately discover their interests. Are they keen on golf, into quiet retreats, a fantasy folly fan, a lover of super hotels, or just fond of losing themselves in a rural richness?

This is a slice of rural north Shropshire between Whitchurch and Market Drayton, which is a treasure trove of surprises. Indeed they do make that sometimes dodgy claim, that Hawkstone Park is unique. With hidden paths which twist and turn, unexpected cliffs, towers, tunnels, caves and grotto petrification in 100 acres of hilly terrain, that's probably fair comment. And although legend tells the tale of two giants building and living in the red castle that is still within the tree-clad slopes of the hotel's grounds, the truth is rather more mundane.

It was Henry de Audley who in the 13th century bought the area of Westune where he built the Red Castle (the name Weston-under-Redcastle survives to this day) and around 500 years later, the Castle and surrounding lands were bought by Sir Rowland Hill, later Lord Hill. His son, Sir Richard, built many of the antiquities and follies which still exist and provide a place of wonder and excitement for the modern day visitor.

A drive to Hodnet Hall Gardens for tea is a splendid way to round off a trip. More than 60 acres of landscaping make these some of the finest gardens in the country (*inset*).

Llanyblodwel and Ruyton XI Towns

'You and I must keep from shame
In London streets, the Shropshire name;
On banks of Thames they must not say
Severn breeds worse men than they.'

A. E. Housman, *XXXVII*

Llanyblodwel doesn't sound remotely as if it's in Shropshire at all. You could hardly get a more Welsh name. But then, you can't get much closer to Shropshire's northern border with Wales than right here.

The village is ancient, an absorbing curiosity for the visitor. The church was originally Norman, but only the south doorway of that early building remains. The rest of St Michael the Archangel is straight Victorian, designed by former vicar John Parker. Only a glorious eccentric could produce a curved tower on an octagonal base and almost child-like stencilling on pillars and ceiling. While

the quaint, 15th-century, black and white Horseshoe Inn is one of the oldest along this part of the Borderland.

William Henry Perry Leslie of Bryn Tanat, a well known musician was asked by the WI to choose a suitable anthem for them. He chose Blake's *Jerusalem*, they sing it still, the world over. Leslie died in 1926, is buried in the churchyard and the handsome lychgate is his memorial.

Today, the river ripples along contentedly and forever beneath Llanyblodwel's 18th-century, sandstone bridge (*opposite*) with its distinctive trio of arches — a gateway to Tanat Valley charm.

Back across the A5 is Ruyton XI Towns which was created in the 13th century by the Fitzalan family and, as the name suggests, is one of the eleven towns established as the Manor of Ruyton. A stone cross (*inset*) stands in the village on the site of the former lock up and an inscription lists the eleven towns that made up the townships.

Ruyton was the long-time home of a grand old lady of her day, Miss Gwynedd LLoyd. Miss LLoyd, a lady-in-waiting to Princess Mary, was truly of another age and woven into the very fabric of Shropshire. She, and her father before her, had lifetime links with the great West Midlands Show and for many years, she was president of the Shropshire Federation of Women's Institutes. Miss LLoyd died in the 1990s well into her own nineties.

Newport

*'I had heard of Miss Havisham up town … as an immensely rich and grim lady who
lived in a large and dismal house barricaded against robbers.'*

Charles Dickens, *Great Expectations*.

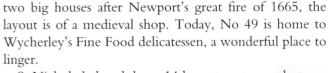

Newport (*opposite*) is one of those old market towns which since it sits on a busy, major road, a lot of people admit to only passing through. And yet, and happily, thousands do park, stroll, browse and shop in this easy, elegant town on the long A41, the Wolverhampton to Whitchurch road. A traditional hub for surrounding farming communities, in its winding, wide main street, black-and-white history lives alongside wonderful hardware and other shops which seem to sell absolutely everything. 'Everything, darlin' is one cheerful shopkeeper's line, 'except what you want!'

The town has some fine frontages (*inset*), with Number 49 in the High Street a good example of Newport's classic past. A slender town house with a Victorian façade, built as an infill between two big houses after Newport's great fire of 1665, the layout is of a medieval shop. Today, No 49 is home to Wycherley's Fine Food delicatessen, a wonderful place to linger.

St Nicholas' church has a 14th-century tower, but was rebuilt in the late 19th century. The A41 snakes along one side of the church, cobbled St Mary's Street on the other. Here, too, is the town's major hotel, the Royal Victoria, one of many in which the great Queen herself is said to have taken refreshment, while Charles Dickens stayed at the former Bear Inn, now Beaumaris House. Dickens based his character Miss Havisham from *Great Expectations* on a woman he met in Newport.

The Barley Mow retains its 'old inn' character and estate agents Davies, White and Perry, founded in 1806, represent old family business. Adams Grammar School is a noted and elegant building and with the Girls' High on the edge of the town, Newport is favoured by parents from much farther afield.

Years after Tuckers shop collapsed, every week the local newspaper reminded readers of the eyesore, to try and shame someone into action. The most famous wreck in Newport has now opened as a smart, new library!

Haughmond Abbey and Attingham Park

*'The landscape park at Attingham remains one of the most
unspoilt examples of Humphry Repton's work.'*

David Brown, National Trust.

Two fine attractions for walkers, browsers, lovers of ruins or admirers of big house grandeur are both now in the care of 21st-century conservationists just a leisurely 15-minute Sunday afternoon drive apart.

Take a walk back to yesteryear at Haughmond Abbey (*opposite*), north of Shrewsbury, through the ruins of the 12th-century Augustinian monastery. Added to during the next 300 years, it was then dissolved and partly demolished in the 1500s with the Dissolution of the Monasteries. A present seven-day English Heritage guardian of the abbey ruins — down a wooded track off the B5062 — swears that she regularly sees the lowly monk in rough brown habit whose job it was to take the waste from the 18-hole reredorter to the large cloister where the monks both grew vegetables and buried their important dead. Linger, absorb a little of the past and you might see him, too.

Then on the quiet drive from Haughmond along winding lanes and flat plains through Uffington village, mull over the timeless peace of an abbey which for so long knew prayer, praise, devotion and finally unspeakable violence. The Battle of Shrewsbury in 1403 was one of the bloodiest in English history and the Abbey was in the thick of it all, taking in the dead and wounded.

Arrive at Attingham Hall, now in the care of the National Trust, for a welcome cup of tea — in the summer season that is. You'd hardly call Atcham a village, more a hamlet, its name a diminutive of Attingham. The church, the only one in Britain dedicated to St Eata, stands alongside the river.

Attingham Hall with its graceful columns, interior gems of decoration and furnishings and Nash picture gallery, was built for the first Lord Berwick. Today Attingham has a fine record as an adult education college and many locals use it most often for jolly dog walking around the splendid grounds and woodland (*inset*).

Lilleshall

*'There is no doubt that resident groups enjoy the peace and solitude
of a stately home in the delightful county of Shropshire.'*

Derek Tremayne, former director of Lilleshall Hall.

Lilleshall is best known to the passer-by for its distinctive hill topped by a memorial to the Duke of Sutherland (*opposite*). But the name is now widely familiar because the National Sports Centre is based at Lilleshall Hall (*inset*), which was built in the early 19th century for the same Duke. He had a fine record of building homes for his farmworkers and many distinctive Duke of Sutherland cottages survive.

But the most fascinating peep at the past is at 12th-century Lilleshall Abbey in a woodland setting along the bottom road. A local guide is said to have seen, even

heard, the ghost of a long-ago monk. The sound of a Georgian chant drifting through the abbey ruins at eventide would not surprise.

With not much of a centre, apart from the cheerful Anvil Stores, Lilleshall has long been a dormitory of nearby market town Newport, and now of the ever-growing Telford stretching out west. But its more distant history lay with the Shropshire coalfields which dominated and supported the east of the county. There are traces of old canals, tunnels and there was once even a blast furnace hereabouts.

You'd never know that today, though, strolling around the village with its mix of smart and quaint cottage homes and gentle, pastoral views over rich and rolling farmland. The origins of St Michael's church are Norman but there may have been a Saxon church on the hill more than 1,300 years ago. St Michael's has a splendid, three-sided stone wall with a cemetery across the road. Now, a field's walk away, sprawls the almost obligatory rural golf club — The Shropshire — just outside the next village of Muxton.

Another modern, if unlikely, sport in this quiet spot, is celebrity spotting. With famous names and faces from football, cricket and athletics often in residence at Lilleshall Hall, there may even be the chance of an autograph!

Shrewsbury — Town of Flowers

*'England is still governed from Langar Rectory, from Shrewsbury School, from
Cambridge with their annexes of the Stock Exchange and solicitors' offices …'*
George Bernard Shaw, 1936.

One of England's finest market towns, Shrewsbury nestles in a sweeping River Severn horseshoe with gateways to two countries, the English and Welsh bridges.

Within its watery boundaries lie crooked medieval streets, 600-year-old black and white timber buildings like Rowley's House Museum which traces a rich history, and a splendid 12th-century castle, now home to a regimental museum.

Gallant soldier Rowland Hill, who fought under Wellington at Waterloo, was born at Prees but elected Member of Parliament for Shrewsbury in 1812. He was overseas at the time, and became a peer in 1814 so never actually sat in the Commons. Lord Hill's real heritage lies at Hawkstone Park but Shrewsbury's 133 foot high pillar topped by his statue, is a landmark and the world's tallest Doric column.

Shrewsbury's most famous son, Charles Darwin, gave the world his theory of evolution by natural selection. Locally, Darwin was named man of the last millennium, and his statue is outside the library (*inset*).

This originally Saxon settlement known as Scrobbesbyrig, is steeped in history, but retains a major 21st-century role. The annual Shropshire and West Midland Agricultural Show — the West Mid — is a major draw, though sadly a victim of foot and mouth disease in 2001, while each August, the Town of Flowers hosts its world famous Flower Show (*opposite*). A floral gem, set in the riverside Quarry and Dingle gardens, it is still linked with the 'nation's head gardener', the late Percy Thrower, TV personality and Shrewsbury's Parks Superintendent for nearly 30 years.

Shrewsbury and its Abbey

'Welcome friend and stranger to this holy place; to this soil where God has been worshipped for over 1,000 years — an unbroken stream of praise and thanksgiving.'

Ian Ross, Vicar of the Abbey Church, 2001.

At Shrewsbury's English boundary stands the Abbey of St Peter and St Paul and parish church of the Holy Cross (*inset*). A name which may not be immediately recognised even by locals but a place which is known and loved by them simply as Shrewsbury Abbey.

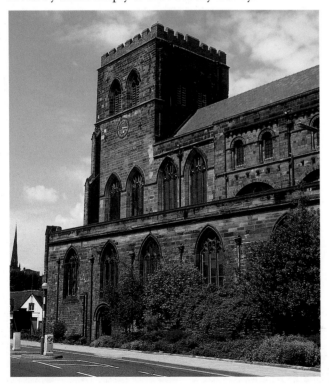

Today's Abbey church goes back to Norman times. But there was a wooden Saxon church on the same site where it is believed St Wulfstan paused to pray when travelling from Worcester to Chester. After William the Conqueror had written his own bit of history, in 1070, he sent a relative, Roger de Montgomerie to the town where a year later he was made Earl of Shrewsbury. Roger's castle building was prolific — including at Shrewsbury itself — and so were his generous gifts to abbeys and priories, chief among these the founding of Shrewsbury Abbey.

In recent times, the fictional *Cadfael* stories brought this great Benedictine Abbey to the attention of a wider, even international audience. The books written by Shropshire's own Ellis Peters, otherwise Edith Pargeter who for most of her life lived at Madeley in the east of the county, and the TV series, were a runaway success.

Nowadays, tourists often take the parking hint, leave their cars safely in Abbey Foregate and enjoy the gentle stroll into the town over the English Bridge (*opposite*) and into Wyle Cop. From the bridge, looking up to the right, the former Royal Salop Infirmary has now been transformed into luxury apartments. But in the hospital's heyday, from its prime spot high above Shrewsbury Town's football pitch, patients who were up to it had an enviable bird's eye view of matches at the Gay Meadow. For free!

Wroxeter

'Before the Roman came to Rye or out to Severn strode,
The rolling English drunkard made the rolling English road.'

G. K. Chesterton (1874–1936), *The Rolling English Road.*

Most of the county's Roman city, Viriconium, still lies below the ground at Wroxeter, alongside that famous London to Holyhead Roman road, Watling Street, the old A5. And just along the same road, a modern day vineyard offers the chance to say cheers to yesteryear, Shropshire style.

The part of the city which has been so painstakingly revealed excites the imagination of archaeologists, historians, visitors and locals alike. And while the cost of complete excavation may be prohibitive, in our time at any rate, at least we know the rest is there. Thanks to the marvels of modern day computer imagery, we also know the remains are much more extensive than originally thought. As the visitor strolls round the ancient ruins, open to the public and with a small museum, it needs only average imagination and a smattering of history to feel the buzz of Roman Britain. This was their fourth largest city and for centuries was occupied peacefully by a thriving and stable community.

Bathing and other ablutions were then much more of a public occasion and the ruins include the remains of the once magnificent public baths (*opposite*), with an indication of how our noble ancestors lived, worked and played 1,900 years ago.

Don't visit the abandoned town without seeing Wroxeter village where people live today. Apart from the excavations — thought to have been pioneered by famous engineer Thomas Telford — there are bits of Roman history all round. Not least, at the now redundant St Andrew's church where part of the north wall (*inset*) is built with stone from the old Roman town. This gem spans the ages, with not only Anglo-Saxon but also Norman and other influences, almost to living memory — its porch is Victorian.

Just along the lane is perhaps the most controversial vineyard in the land. The owner, David Millington, fought an eight-year battle with local council planners, finally winning a Court of Appeal case in 2000, to sell his wine. The dispute largely hinged on whether production of the wine was agricultural or industrial.

The Wrekin

'All Friends Round the Wrekin.'

A traditional Shropshire toast which is used all over the world wherever Salopians gather.

Do the origins of the Wrekin and the Ercall owe more to legend and myth than geology? The romantics among us may like to think so.

The Wrekin, the highest point on the east Shropshire landscape (*opposite* and *inset*), stands over 1,300 feet above patchwork countryside, a rambling couple of miles west of Wellington. The gloriously eccentric, wooden Forest

Glen at the foot of the Wrekin hosted generations of celebratory dinners with glasses raised in the famous toast, *All Friends Round the Wrekin*. The building has been re-erected in the Blists Hill open air museum at Coalport.

Generations of locals and visitors have climbed the Wrekin, squeezed through the needle's eye rock viewing point and marvelled at the panorama of surrounding counties.

The views are fact, what of the origins? Try this — a mayor of Shrewsbury once upset a giant with a massive temper. The giant took revenge by scooping up a spade full of Welsh soil and heading off towards Shrewsbury to dump it in the River Severn, flood the town and drown its people. But Mr Giant missed a turn and wandered on eastwards towards Wellington. He was tired by now, put down his earth and scraped the mud off his boots. Then he asked a cobbler going home with a bag full of shoes for mending, directions to Shrewsbury. The cobbler did business with Shrewsbury, so he showed the giant a shoe full of holes and said he'd worn it out walking back from there. It sounded like an awfully long way to a tired giant who accepted defeat and went home. Leaving behind a spade full of earth — the Wrekin. And the scrapings from his boot — Ercall Hill.

A gentle tale to ponder on a dreamy day up there, at rest in the heather with one of Britain's most beautiful shires in perfect miniature at your feet!

Telford

'When Captain Webb the Dawley man,
Captain Webb from Dawley,
Came swimming along the old canal
That carried the bricks to Lawley.'

Sir John Betjeman, *A Shropshire Lad.*

That solid east Shropshire settlement of Dawley knew about achievement. In August 1875, its famous son, Captain Matthew Webb became the first man to swim the English Channel. The zig-zag 40-mile route took him 22 hours. Bravado got the good captain in the end, when he drowned on 24th July 1883 trying to swim the rapids and whirlpool beneath the Niagara Falls.

Webb's Dawley was the old pit and steel environment, and while that high street might still be just about recognisable, today's wider Telford has massive shopping complexes, the International Tennis Centre, multi-national businesses, big hotel chains and soaring buildings catching light at every angle. All rose like 20th-century phoenixes from the ashes of yesteryear when in the early days of Telford Development Corporation, a planner waved his hand across the wreck of industrial heritage and described a new dream — Dawley New Town.

In the 1960s, a robust injection of planning and cash, and a vision of a bustling future, laid the foundations for a town in the traditions of the post-war garden cities and named after Thomas Telford, Shropshire's first county surveyor. He was not only one of our greatest ever engineers but a fine builder of bridges, roads and canals. Shropshire's rich heritage has many such examples, as well as churches and a famous iron aqueduct.

Boscobel and Tong

'We went that night from Worcester to a place called White Ladies, hard by Tong Castle by the advice of Mr Giffard.'

King Charles II on his escape to Shropshire after being beaten at the Battle of Worcester.

Boscobel House (*opposite*) is described as a modest, timber-framed building, surely little disturbed by the tumult of national events. Yet the house, flanked by open fields near to Tong, grips the imagination.

Because for one, brief shining moment 350 years ago

during England's Civil War, Boscobel starred in the grand order of events which changed our history. It saved the life of a king. Charles II took refuge here in 1651 after his army had been battered at Worcester. He first fled to a house at White Ladies then to Boscobel House, where he hid in a tiny space beneath a trapdoor as his enemies closed in. Finally the King was taken outside to climb high into a tree, famous to this day as the Royal Oak.

Now, the house is in the care of English Heritage and open to a still fascinated public. The oak stands 150 yards away, surrounded by iron fencing. Hearing the part the oak had played in preserving the King's safety, 17th-century souvenir hunters stripped and damaged it so the present tree may actually be a descendant of the original.

Tong itself nurses an amazing history of power and influence, with the remains of a Norman castle, a 15th-century Chantry College and the present impressive church standing high above the main road and dating from about the same time. It is packed with effigies, tombs and monuments to the nobility (*inset*) and is of even more interest to many because the remains of Charles Dickens' Little Nell are also said to lie there.

Now, Dickens did visit Tong but seemingly the legend of Little Nell's 'grave' may owe more to a cunning church verger who rightly judged tourist interest.

Broseley

*'The project which was to culminate in the building of the Iron Bridge began
in September 1775 when a group of interested people met at the house of
Abraham Cannadine in Broseley.'*

Historian Dr Barrie Trinder

Broseley is one of the old east Shropshire towns. Four hundred years ago it was a busy and successful industrial area, closely linked to thriving Coalbrookdale on the other side of the Severn and so, very much part of the early Industrial Revolution.

Already a thriving industrial settlement by the beginning of the 17th century, over the next 200 years the town developed into a major area for coal mining, iron and earthenware manufacture. In the early 1600s, a crude, short but efficient wooden line, for industrial use, became the first railway in Shropshire. The famous Iron Bridge built in 1779 linked Broseley with Coalbrookdale and founded Ironbridge itself.

That early industrial activity helped give Broseley a character all of its own. Building styles include Georgian elegance, Victorian workers' cottages and, now, much 20th-century estate building. The surprisingly large All Saints church dominates the eastern end and in the long and winding main street with its traditional shops (*inset*), a neatly grassed square houses the War Memorial.

Coalport and other china displays at the Cumberland Hotel are impressive and Broseley's once thriving ancillary business of clay pipe making (for smoking) also led to some fascinating collections. In the heyday of the world famous

Coalport china industry, many workers at the bustling, blazing kilns acquired valuable collections, now passed on to family or eagerly snapped up in local antique shops.

The old riverside Coalport factory, just minutes away from Broseley (*opposite*), stands testament to its roots and is one of the most popular museums in this cradle of the Industrial Revolution.

Ironbridge

'It's gone the full circle, it was the ninth wonder of the world in the 1780s.
Artists and writers flocked to see it, all we knew was that it was the first iron bridge
and that was that.'

Local historian, Ken Jones in the late 20th century.

It was named after the world's first iron bridge (*inset*), triumphantly erected in 1779 and still spanning the River Severn. Those days of thriving, bustling trade when the river was king, its banks dotted with businesses of the time, dozens of pubs and more than a few brothels, have given way to a quieter hillside village, a mecca for tourists and for those longing to live in this now picturesque, beating heart of the Industrial Revolution.

Meander riverside where old Harry Rogers made his coracles, entertained with river tales and sent his little craft, shaped like half a walnut, bobbing along the Severn. Half a mile upstream to Dale End, turn right at the famous Merrythought Teddy Bear Museum and wind less than a mile up the breathtakingly impressive wooded valley to Coalbrookdale.

The whole area offers a range of special living history events as well as hands-on activities for children. There is no other place on earth like it and it is now part of a World Heritage Site.

It was at Coalbrookdale, in what is now the first of the Gorge museums, that the Darby family honed the smelting technique to make the building of an iron bridge possible. And for soccer fans, the delightfully named Paradise was childhood home of the legendary Billy Wright!

In Ironbridge itself, every road climbs or ducks and dives, becomes an alleyway or a passage, presents what seems like a million steps to shoppers with many carrier bags. And talking of steps, if you walk up to St Luke's church from the grand Victorian square, you'll conquer 110 of them. If you turn the other way and cross the recently restored bridge, you'll be walking into history.

Harley and Sheinton

'Fortunate too is the man who has come to know the gods of the countryside.'
Virgil, *Georgics, ii 493.*

Around the black-and-white and much admired tourist market town of Much Wenlock, there are delightful villages, snatched and prettily placed like patchwork pieces on this most lovely stretch of Shropshire's rolling plains. One such village is little Harley (*opposite*), a couple of miles from the town, drifting gently away off the steep A458 Cressage to Wenlock road.

There are several very smart homes hereabouts, some still providing work for the thatcher, others fine gentleman's residences and a number of imposing more modern houses, all eagerly sought after. The church of St Mary, a 19th-century rebuild, retains its medieval tower and houses some fascinating and locally-produced stained glass. The panorama is of a pleasant rural landscape at the foot of a rugged, forested slab of Wenlock Edge, in easy reach of a few pubs of good repute. Driving up the hill from the village on a winter's day, massive icicles cling like stalactites to the cliff-like rock face. Below, all is placid, peaceful and quietly content.

Another little gem on this side of the crown of the hill is Sheinton (pronounced shine-ton), (*inset*), just over a mile away, the other side of sprawling Cressage village. Its roots are deeply embedded in Anglo-Saxon and Norman history and once one of its masters was Ralph of Mortimer, lover of Edward II's wife, Isabella.

Winding your way into the village, the central focus is what it traditionally always was, the church, blessed with the name of not just one but two saints. St Peter and St Paul's stands on its own little green hillock, approached through a startlingly bright blue gate, its frontage of ancient gravestones standing at crazy angles, once-fond inscriptions long since gone. A place which has a magnetic grip on the escapee from a frantic world.

Snailbeach

'A time there was, 'ere England's grief began
When every rood of ground maintained its man;
For him light labour spread her wholesome store,
Just gave what life required, but gave no more.'
        Oliver Goldsmith, *The Deserted Village*.

Even the Romans took lead from Snailbeach, the largest of the Shropshire lead mines (*opposite*). And in later years, at the end of the 1800s, the flourishing mines were the centre for the largest lead mining complex in Europe. Up to 500 men once worked there, hard to

visualise in these quieter, calmer days.

Yet apart from a smattering of tiny farms, almost all the settlements around Snailbeach were spawned from lead mining. Part of the area is now a fascinating open museum, some buildings have been restored, others are still in that state of glorious ruin from which so much of our past is eventually rescued (*inset*). In December 2000 the restored mine site was officially opened by Sir Neil Cossins, former director of the Ironbridge Gorge Museum Trust, now chairman of English Heritage and still a Shropshire resident.

The mineral railway lives on in the narrow-gauge tracks of the line which ran between Pontesbury and Minsterley. Old 'pigs' of Roman lead have been found as well as even more evidence of past lead mining history. Those early miners would work surface outcrops of ore and one such outcrop was recently discovered above Snailbeach. As they made progress, they followed the ore into the hill by driving levels and sinking shafts.

But romance as well as lead flourished hereabouts. This was very much Mary Webb country. And the old Lordshill Baptist church up above the former mining reservoir, was featured in the film version of *Gone to Earth*, the best known of the evocative works from Shropshire's famous authoress.

Offa's Dyke

'What a relaxed life is that which flees the worldly clamour
and follows the hidden path …'

Fray Luis de Leon, *Vida Retirada.*

On a bright and breezy day when scudding clouds are only little ones and the great panorama of sky touches earth many miles from where you are, there are few finer spots to stand and stare along the county's border with Wales. This is Offa's Dyke. The amazing 176-mile stretch of track, scrub, incline and breath-snatching climb which has mesmerised walkers over the years is still there for the enjoying.

Of course, much of it isn't in Shropshire at all. And that which is, teeters over the county's edge — just as intended. Offa, ruler of the Saxon kingdom of Mercia, had the ditch and earth rampart constructed in the 8th century to mark out the boundary 'twixt his land and Wales. It also proved a great defence asset running as it does from the Severn to the Dee, from Sedbury Cliffs near Chepstow in the south of Wales to Prestatyn in the north. Shropshire's is the relatively short slice in the middle. But you can walk most of it. Gaps tend to be in those areas which, in common with much of the borderland, were once thickly forested.

The path follows about 60 miles of the dyke which is still visible. In spring to early summer, wild flowers are marvellous, from bluebell-carpeted woodland to early wild orchids.

There is something deep inside human beings which responds to great outcrops of rock, roughly fashioned circles, any ancient landscape which might have housed even the crudest altar or is open to the rising or the setting sun. Such places speak of our ancestry in the most basic way. And so it is at nearby Stapeley Hill and Mitchell's Fold (*inset*). The legend talks of a witch, a fairy queen and a magical white cow producing unlimited milk in times of famine. The reality is more likely a place of pagan religious rites well before Christianity and since in Shropshire, the word 'fold' was used for farmyard, is that what this place could well have been? Where a farmer milked a magic cow? Dream on!

Stiperstones

'We have sought it, we have sought the golden arrow
Bright the sally-willows sway.
Two and two by paths low and narrow,
Arm in crook along the mountain way.'

Mary Webb in her first book *The Golden Arrow*,
set in the Stiperstone hill country.

Little children quiver at the name but still insist on being brought here. To this bleak and breezy outpost with a magnificent view, known with a delicious sense of fear as the mighty Devil's Chair.

Flung along the side of the rambling Stiperstones Hills down in south Shropshire, it is the biggest of a number of rocky outcrops snaking like a crazy backbone down this lonely, hilly range (*opposite*). When the weather is grim, the Devil's Chair can loom like a sinister presence and it has its share of legends. They include an annual gathering of ghosts, the claim that this is the burial place of Wild Edric, and that sheep are inexplicably terrified if they stray close to the Devil's Chair during darkness.

Though there is much more to it than that: this is a place of rugged beauty, of valleys and moorlands, remote reminders of yesteryear and for many, an enveloping refuge from the fast moving 21st century. There are no commuter treadmills in these parts! Long ago, Shropshire authoress Mary Webb found much inspiration here. Born at Leighton near Shrewsbury in 1881, her lifelong passion was this south-western corner of her county.

There are magnificent views. Like those of the brooding Stiperstones on approach, and the splendid panorama unfolding in all directions once you are up

there, striding in the steps of forefathers who loved and worked these ancient plains. Look east on a good day and you will see that other, bigger range of Shropshire's southern hills, the Long Mynd (*inset*). Old and welcome hostelries scattered around the villages provide basic creature comforts. But just for a while, the Stiperstones visitor can experience what going back to nature really means.

Much Wenlock

Ancient Much Wenlock is a rare mix of all those things which tourists love: history, character, wonderful stories, and tales of sporting derring-do. To add to its attractions, the Wenlock Olympian Trail was officially opened in spring 2001 to celebrate the influence of Much Wenlock's Dr William Penny Brookes on the revival of the Ancient Greek games.

The trail, inspired by the Wenlock Olympian Society, takes the visitor on a highly informative guided tour of the town. It was appropriate that the launch day started at the 17th-century former coaching inn, the Gaskell Arms Hotel where Dr Brookes would have spoken to the crowds during the opening of the original Games more than 150 years ago. And where he sternly warned that the penalty for disorderly or drunken behaviour on the streets could be as much as five shillings!

The 21st-century ceremony (*inset*) keeps to the spirit of the original games with a procession led along the town's High Street by modern day Shropshire Olympic athletes carrying the Olympic torch.

The refurbished Museum and Tourist Information Centre in the old Memorial Hall on the picturesque little Square has a selection of memorabilia from the Wenlock Olympian Society collection, including a computer database with selected archives.

But this wonderful little town also treasures a black and white 1540 Guildhall (*opposite*), and the historic Talbot Inn whose origins go back to 1361 and whose present timber framed building dates from the 1600s. In 1949, the Mary Webb film *Gone to Earth* with Jennifer Jones and George Cole was partly filmed in its courtyard. The first stone for the Corn Market was laid in 1852 and the approach to the Town Council and library is now beneath its pillared canopy. The monument and clock in the Square erected in honour of Queen Victoria's Diamond Jubilee in 1897, was refurbished in 1993 to mark 40 years of our own Queen's reign.

The Long Mynd

'There, somewhere, nor-nor-east from me
Was Shropshire, where I longed to be.
Ercall and Mynd,
Severn and Wrekin, you and me.'

John Masefield.

From every direction the Long Mynd dominates. If you should leave Church Stretton by car, the most direct route is up the Burway. Direct it may be but it is also narrow with a sheer drop and most worryingly, two-way traffic. Perhaps not for the faint hearted behind the wheel!

But there are less alarming options, easily identified on a good local map. And once up there the experience pays for all with views which roll back the very horizon of

heaven. Looking east to brooding Caer Caradoc (*opposite* and *inset*) across the A49 highway, stirs the most exhilarating feeling of truly being at one with the hills.

Though the Mynd has had its less quiet moments — the 1st Artillery Corps (later the 1st Shropshire and Staffordshire Artillery Volunteers) once had an artillery practice range here.

Anyone who has ever 'slipped the surly bands of earth' to glide silently and majestically over hill and woodland, hollow and mountain track, will understand the draw of the Midland Gliding Club which is also based on the Long Mynd. From the air, the range's deep and narrow valleys are scooped out like the track of a giant's finger through cake icing. These 'batches' are said to have been caused by massive sheets of ice which simply gouged them out in the big meltdown at the end of the Ice Age.

All far distant from these days, when for the walker, memories of the Mynd are of the views, a brisk breeze on your face and the chance to pick juicy wild berries in season.

Across the way, dominant Caer Caradoc itself is the most striking signpost on the Stretton boundaries. Once the home of ancient tribes as a fortified hill town, it is 1,500 craggy feet high but well worth the testing climb.

Church Stretton

'Not only has the climate a generally tonic and invigorating effect but it also has the valuable quality of exercising a somewhat tranquillizing influence on the nervous system and circulation.'

From the 1912 official handbook of the
Church Stretton Advancement Association.

The former spa town of Church Stretton (*opposite* and *inset*) is set not only in the heart of the south Shropshire Hills country, but in another age. A quieter, gentler, more courteous time when shops were shops and not massive out-of-town complexes, banks were banks and not craft centres, churches were churches and not up-market homes.

In truth, along with the rest of the world, many things have changed but Church Stretton still presents its own illusion of a kinder yesteryear. Set in a long valley between the Long Mynd and the Stretton Hills, it has a Victorian feel, yet along with the rest of the area has some lovely black and white timber buildings and is home to specialist shops, old hostelries and charming tea venues.

There has been a market here since the time of King John and one is still held in the pretty little Square. The Domesday Book records that along with neighbouring All Stretton and Little Stretton, it was originally known as Stratun. And as with other parts of rolling south Shropshire, writers and artists are drawn to this place. Despite straddling the feet of so many hillsides, the town centre is mostly flat and easily accessible. St Laurence's church stands on the site of an earlier, Saxon church and has a Norman nave.

The Long Mynd Hotel high above the town is a mecca for visitors with its breathtaking views. It's one of those places which from the A49 far below, travellers look way up on an ever-rising hillside and wonder: 'How on earth did that get there?' Who can be surprised then that 100 years ago, London posters proclaimed Church Stretton as the Highlands of England! Even a simple stroll around the town offers peace and unsurpassable scenery. And venture only a little farther afield for paradise on earth.

The Long Mynd above Church Stretton

'My hands were so numb with cold as to be nearly useless. Icicles likewise had formed
about my eyes and eyebrows and my hair had frozen into a solid block of ice.'

The Reverend Donald Carr, *A Night in the Snow.*

Not surprisingly, Carding Mill Valley attracts most of the visitors to the Strettons. It is an easy walk with sheep-dotted hillsides powering away on either side and if you must, you can drive your car up its length, 'park prettily' and then stroll or maybe climb a bit. The Long Mynd awaits you!

Beneath its covering of richly purple heather and crew-cut grass (*opposite*), lie some of the oldest rocks in Britain, many hidden forever, several miles down. The walks and views are unsurpassable and call locals and visitors back again and again for exercise, revival and the renewal of the human spirit.

Ashes Hollow for instance (*inset*), provides a good, off-track outing which is not too difficult. And the Long Mynd offers a range of walks for everyone from toddlers to experienced hikers who demand a challenge every time. Though heed the advice that hill walking demands attention to fitness, weather and equipment.

The tale of the Rev Donald Carr's battle with the Long Mynd in January 1865 is chronicled in the little book *A Night in the Snow*. Every Sunday the vicar walked from Woolastaton to pastoral duty at the tiny church of St Margaret, Ratlinghope (pronounced Rachup), his route high across the northern edge of the Long Mynd. On that long January night, he fought an amazing battle against blizzards, changing winds and deep ravines. Rev Carr somehow survived, arriving home 22 dark and icy hours later. Let that be a warning!

Bridgnorth

'I really do see Bridgnorth as becoming the Salzburg of Shropshire.'
Flamboyant musician John Reid when he established
the English Haydn Festival in 1990.

Bridgnorth (*opposite*) can rival many cities of music in charm. And over this past decade, the now annual English Haydn Festival in early summer has drawn visitors locally and from every continent. It is based at St Leonard's church (*inset*), with its pretty square of almshouses, cottages and an inviting stretch of lawn for the festival supper marquee.

Split-level Bridgnorth has long been a visitor attraction, sitting on a gentle stretch of the Severn, surrounded by exciting cliffs and caves. There is a sandstone drop of more than 100 feet between the two 'towns' and you can drive round the system or take the winding walk through narrow streets. But for more than a century, the Bridgnorth Cliff Railway has carried shoppers and visitors between the riverside Low Town and the busy shopping and business centre of High Town. Once operated by a water ballast system, today the cars have electric winding engines.

Halfway up the Stoneway Steps, Bridgnorth's own theatre operates out of an old chapel. What else could it be called but The Theatre on the Steps?

The reopening of the Severn Valley Railway brought more visitors to the prosperous market town with its antiques, craft and traditional shops, wide variety of restaurants and hostelries — many charmingly old.

Much of medieval Bridgnorth was destroyed by 17th-century fire, though the fine, timbered Bishop Percy's house of 1581 still stands in the Cartway, the castle remains are 12th-century and there are some splendid Georgian properties. Astrologer Francis Moore, born in Bridgnorth in 1657, found much wider fame as Old Moore of the annual almanac. While the creator of Jeeves, P. G. Wodehouse, lived in the village of Stableford five miles out of Bridgnorth for about seven years. He was fond of the area and often used it as a setting for his books.

The Severn Valley Railway

'The traveller said: 'I want to go
to Shropshire if you please,
By first class train where I can quite
relax and take my ease.'

Jack Insall, *What's in a Name?*

It's the stuff of which little boys' dreams are made, where *The Railway Children* comes to life. Never mind the gripes of daily commuters, for thousands of visitors and railway enthusiasts who each year take the spectacular 16-mile journey from Bridgnorth (*opposite*) in Shropshire to Kidderminster, just over the border with Worcestershire, this is a love affair.

A proper choo-choo, puff-puff, clouds of steam job. The sort of train travel which old people remember with nostalgia and young people will never know. Except for

wonderful conservation projects like the Severn Valley Railway. Wide eyed little lads clutch their prized Thomas the Tank Engine, and the hands of equally excited dads, to take a magical trip down the line.

For all generations, this gentle drift into the past on a journey which mostly follows the course of the River Severn is a delight. And as the network of rural roads and lanes falls away, there are some fabulous views only ever seen from the railway. Not least from the spectacular 200 foot single-span Victoria Bridge, high in the valley above the meandering Severn. Stop off at any of the old world country stations down the line, all of them close to local villages and all offering a gentle riverside stroll, then pick up a later train. This is an all-year round affair with lots of specials — like seasonal trips with Santa.

Severn Valley trains regularly appear on television and their charm puts them high on the visitor list of what to do in Shropshire. One of the pretty stations on the route at Highley (*inset*), is well used to the attention of film makers. The old coal mining village itself, though, is now one of the biggest in the county, its rows of terraced miners' cottages joined by the facilities of a small town. For local charm, stick to the steam train where the standard gauge, full size railway line is the gateway to a journey into yesteryear preserved for today.

Bishop's Castle

'It was drunk in honeysuckle, all the clocks had stopped many years ago, the hedges brushed against the ancient carriages.'

A local description as the neglected branch line between Bishop's Castle and Lydbury finally closed in 1935.

Of Bishop's Castle in south Shropshire (*opposite*), you can fairly say that it's miles from anywhere. Once England's smallest borough in her largest inland county, it is 25 rural miles from the county town of Shrewsbury, a stone's throw from the Welsh border. It was founded in the 8th century when a Saxon landowner cured of palsy was so grateful that he gave estates to the Bishop of Hereford. The castle, finished in 1100, was built by the bishops and a town created to serve it. In the 17th century, the castle was rebuilt in stone, and the 1719 Castle Hotel stands on the historic site. The borough charter was granted in 1573, during the first Elizabethan age, and the town badge is dated 1609.

The church, dedicated to St John the Baptist, was built in 1219, rebuilt in 1860, is bigger than you expect and has some fine Victorian stained glass. Near the 18th-century Town Hall, one of the oldest houses is also the most curious. The upper floors of the House on Crutches (*inset*) are supported on posts creating a pathway underneath. Now owned by the Old Castle Land Trust, the house is a local history museum.

The railway trip which once connected Bishop's Castle to Craven Arms was scenic beauty at its best, crossing the River Onny no fewer than six times. And a delightful story records the ambitious branch line created from nearby Lydbury in 1865 which had money troubles the moment its backing fell through. The company had to pay massive interest charges and a year later, went bankrupt. But amazingly, a sympathetic Receiver helped the community keep the line open with little investment and ancient rolling stock — which they did until 1935.

Corve Dale

'Yet still on mornings such as these
The mirage shifts our channelled course.
Streams run uphill above the trees;
The hero on enchanted horse
Opens incredible doors.'

Robert Gittings, *The Fairy Tale.*

The Corve Dale (*opposite*) is a magical sweep of pastoral Shropshire bounded by Wenlock Edge on one side and the Clee Hills on the other. Travellers from Bridgnorth or Much Wenlock down towards Ludlow must take care not to be overwhelmed by this swathe of breathtakingly beautiful land around them and so find themselves doing a touch of off-road driving.

Corve Dale — the name is an easy one to understand. This is the land of the River Corve and one of the most spectacular dales and valleys, edges and hillsides. Its

hemline is dotted with pretty little villages, farms and surprisingly sophisticated hostelries as well as traditional rural pubs.

Near the junction with both the main but winding roads to Ludlow as the land opens up to the south, lies the village of Shipton, distinguished by handsome Shipton Hall standing proud beyond immaculate lawns. The Elizabethan house was built for Richard Lutwyche, eventually becoming a dowry for his daughter.

Motte (a mound marking the site of castle or camp) and bailey (an open space enclosed by a fortification) remains are scattered down the Dale and there are tales of more. At Munslow, for instance, the Wenlock limestone village which gazes away towards the Brown Clee. While its little sister just down the road, Aston Munslow, boasts the widely known black and white timbered Swan Inn, first winner of the local newspaper's Perfect Pub competition.

Diddlebury (*inset*) is a village of old stone. The Fair Rosamund lived at Corfham Castle (its remains in a field just south-east of the village), her fame lying in winning the attentions of a king — Henry II.

Glebe Farm, a rather splendid abode with both stone and timbered gables, is now an award winning, period guest house, Corve Dale style!

Broome and Clunton

'Oh to be in England
Now that April's there,
And whoever wakes in England
Sees some morning, unaware,
That the lowest boughs on the brushwood sheaf
Round the elm tree bole are in tiny leaf.'

Robert Browning, *Home Thoughts from Abroad.*

Clunton is not much more than a hamlet a couple of miles east of Clun. While a little farther east and nearer to Craven Arms, the settlement of Broome in the Vale of Clun meanders along the road as though she's rather lost her way but doesn't mind a bit.

And nor will the visitor mind if hereabouts an intended trip turns into a wandering sort of day. Because around these places is as close as you get to the rural heart of Shropshire as the farmland above Broome (*opposite*) demonstrates. Broome itself occupies a mere few hundred yards of roadway distinguished by the Engine and Tender pub, complete with camping and caravan site inviting the traveller to pause awhile. Apart from a few terraced houses with smart, rouged-up fronts and a rusty little bridge over the road, the tiny hamlet is now more or less smart new dwellings, smart country living with mod cons.

Except, that is, for the railway station. But surely not still used? Well, perhaps … Engine and Tender — Remember? Used and confirmed by chance. On a sunny spring morning, curiosity was satisfied when a drive alongside the track revealed the grand sight of a Great Scenic Railways of Cornwall carriage just pulling away.

Back on the winding lane above Clunton (*inset*), nothing stirs in this little settlement. But there have been changes, if not many and not swift. The roadside 1870 Primitive Methodist chapel in grey stone is now The Old Spice Works. And carrying on just round the next bend, which to choose — Ditches Hill Iron Age Fort to the right or Clunton Coppice Nature Reserve to the left? Decisions, decisions. Ah well, perhaps a glass of something long and cool in the Crown Inn instead as you meditate on the altogether gentler pace of life.

Stokesay Castle and Craven Arms

*'Stokesay Castle, Together with all Barnes, Stables, outhouses and buyldings
belonging to the same ...'*

A description of the fine wedding settlement
Charles Baldwyn made on his son, Samuel, in 1648.

Sitting as it does just off the Stretton to Ludlow road, Stokesay Castle (*opposite* and *inset*) is the finest and best preserved 13th-century fortified manor house in England, now cared for by English Heritage.

Stokesay itself dates back almost to the Norman Conquest but there was no Domesday mention of a castle though there was a mill and a beekeeper! Important wool merchant, Lawrence of Ludlow, built the manor house as a particularly fine home and it has barely changed in more than 700 years. Although under threat, it survived the Civil War and was carefully restored in the 1800s. Not only is there much to marvel at inside its medieval walls and an audio tour to bring history alive, but with its timber-framed Jacobean gatehouse, the complex is just so very pretty. And its past is fascinating.

In peaceful meadowland, alongside the equally interesting parish church, park in a field and then let the tranquil moment take over. Idyllic!

Less than a mile away, Craven Arms is a rural town sprawling comfortably either side of the busy but picturesque A49. The Craven Arms Hotel, built around 1800 by the Earl of Craven as a coaching inn for travellers on the turnpike roads, gave the town its name.

Today, many travellers to and from Clun, Shrewsbury, Much Wenlock and Ludlow, pass through. But too often that's all they do — pass through.

Which is a shame. This is a busy, sunny natured town that has a tradition of thriving markets, railways and agriculture.

Burwarton and Bitterley

'Ancient men on Brown Clee Hill
Toiled from break of day;
The tramp of nailed boots echoes still,
A long, lost world away.'

Anon.

Both the main roads snaking out of Ludlow to Much Wenlock and Bridgnorth are dotted with a fascinating collection of villages, hamlets, settlements and interesting pathways leading to who knows where.

Burwarton is one of those villages, though more substantial than some. And particularly interesting since it has been owned for several generations by the Boyne family. Their handsome Burwarton Hall (traditional home of Lord Boyne) nestles in parkland on the eastern slopes of the Brown Clee Hill, and other properties are equally as distinguished in their own way, including the Hall's solid, stone-built former Dower House which is now in private hands.

And as is the case in so many areas, St Lawrence's church which was built in 1876 alongside earlier ruins and became redundant in 1976, has now been deconsecrated to emerge as another private home.

The village was created in an area rich with forest and scrubland and to this day, lovers of forestry find it magnetic. The trees of Burwarton include a splendid, copper beech avenue while ancient yews mark out some of the area's old roads, once used by drovers taking stock to the Brown Clee for grazing. The Burwarton show (*opposite*) is also a popular event.

Nearby Bitterley village (*inset*) is equally interesting with a varied collection of historical buildings. Bitterley Court is dated about 1700 with wonderful Jacobean rooms but a Georgian facade. The local school which dates from the 16th century as a grammar school, was opened up in the 1870s to provide elementary schooling for all, but kept its grammar school title until as recently as 1958. And of more recent vintage is the village hall, called Bitterley Hut simply because it was originally used as an army hut.

Clun

'Widow'd wife and married maid,
Betrothed, betrayer and betray'd.'

Sir Walter Scott, *The Betrothed.*

Clun is just one of that conglomeration of names which fascinate and tongue tie. Team it with Clunton, Clunbury and Clungunford, not to mention Aston on Clun and Newcastle on Clun, and you have a whole south Shropshire family. You also have the essence of those timeless, languid words from A. E. Housman's epic *The Shropshire Lad.* For example — 'Clunton and Clunbury, Clungunford and Clun are the quietest places under the sun,' wrote the poet who so immortalised the county and yet was actually a Worcestershire lad.

But Housman is a good example of so many down the years who discovered this shire, perhaps the land of his blue remembered hills, and never let it go. And so into Clun, the place re-named Oniton by an admirer, E. M. Forster, in his novel *Howard's End.* The stark remains of its castle (*opposite*), a small Marcher fortress built around 1150 by the Norman, Robert de Say are sited on a rocky outcrop on the edge of the village. The castle is thought to have featured in Sir Walter Scott's novel, *The Betrothed.*

The River Clun not only flows through the meadow around the castle but it also slices through the village with the two halves joined by an original 15th-century bridge (*inset*). Indeed, Clun is well known for this bridge alone.

Cross it after leaving the castle and passing through the tiny square, and you'll soon reach the hillside church of St George, thought to have been built on the site of yet another Iron Age fort.

The memorial tablets at crazy angles in the ancient graveyard have a glorious look of Dickensian decay. But close to the church porch are several newer and distinctive headstones in steel grey slate. Beneath one of them lies the author and playwright who no longer looks back in anger but rests in peace. After spending his final days happily in Clun, John Osborne now spends his eternity in its churchyard.

Vale of Clun

'Mine be a cot beside the hill;
A beehive's hum shall soothe my ear;
A willowy brook that turns a mill,
With many a fall shall linger near.'

Samuel Rogers

This south-western corner of Shropshire (*opposite* and *inset*) is a wonderful mix of valleys and old roads, of bright, rippling rivers and daunting hillsides, of ancient forts and historic churches.

Pause at Aston-on-Clun for example where the legendary Arbor Tree, a rare black poplar, was said to be the sole survivor of those decorated by King Charles II to celebrate the restoration of the monarchy on 29th May 1666. The tree was dressed on Arbor Day 1786 for the marriage of Squire Marston of Oaker to Mary Carter of Sibdon who left money and an instruction for it to be dressed annually. Today, the motley collection of international flags, which sprout like extra branches from the present tree, inevitably becomes muddy and sad from passing traffic. Nice custom, though.

Names like Shelderton, Twitchen and Chapel Lawn (on the River Redlake which only lurches into a river when rain comes down from the hills) sound much as they are — quiet, rural and idyllic.

But talking of names, what are we to make of the unlikely sounding New Invention? You may be told that the place was so named after an ingenious blacksmith put the shoes of soldiers' horses on back to front so that the enemy thought the local cavalry had gone in the opposite direction. On the other hand it's apparently common for a new explanation of the name to be regularly invented, hence ... New Invention?

Clun itself once lay at the heart of the Forest of Clun where red deer roamed and the king had the hunting rights. Now, building and charcoal industries have taken their modern day toll.

Ludlow

Ludlow (*opposite*) is a splendid southern gem in Shropshire's crown. It has history, elegance, architecture, a town-centre castle and a wealth of interesting crafts, galleries, antiques and alternative lifestyles.

What's more, this traditional market town with its snakes and ladders system of roads from hilly, winding lanes to steep, sweeping boulevards flanked by superb town houses, is set in a panorama of breathtaking landscapes, views and the pretty River Teme.

Sounds poetic, it is poetic. The 11th-century castle dominates this Marches town and is the stunning, natural setting for the annual, internationally known Ludlow Festival when a Shakespeare play is centrepiece for a fortnight of high-quality art, music, drama and more.

Arthur, King Henry VII's eldest son, and his wife, Catherine, lived at Ludlow Castle. Arthur died, Catherine moved to London and married his brother, Henry. Meet King Henry VIII and Catherine of Aragon. Rich castle history. But nor must the visitor miss the impressive church of St. Laurence with its landmark tower which breathes a century-spanning story of its own.

Ludlow's roots go back nearly 1,000 years when the medieval settlement began as a planned Norman town. Its market in the square outside the castle gates, remains an attraction and a practical trading place for local producers. Intricately carved timbers on the ancient frontage of The Feathers Hotel (*inset*), have helped make it one of the most familiar buildings. Dated 1603, it is in a romantic time warp, joined by a number of other inns and hostelries which have served Ludlow's fathers, their fathers' fathers and generations before them. Who, then, can be surprised that while the body of the hapless Prince Arthur rests at Worcester, his heart remains in Ludlow. At peace, under an English heaven.

Cleobury Mortimer

'Upon man for his mysdedes, the merciment he taxeth.
And for to knowe kyndely, it comseth bi myght,
And in the herte, there is the hevede and the heigh welle.'

From *Piers the Plowman* by 14th-century poet, William Langland,
said to have been born in Cleobury Mortimer.

Hardly a village, but a small town of some rural character, Cleobury Mortimer (*opposite*) lies on the edge of Shropshire's border with Worcestershire. And rather nearer to Kidderminster than its major south Shropshire neighbours of Bridgnorth and Ludlow.

If the Georgian influence adds to the town's attraction, a probe into its history proves absorbing. The present Childe's School, for instance, stands on the site of the 12th-century castle built by Ralph de Mortimer.

And thanks to the foresight of Robert Earl of Dudley, it was in these parts that well before the Industrial Revolution burst forth more generally in Shropshire, a charcoal furnace was built in the 16th century to smelt iron ore recovered in the area. Indeed, until the late 1800s, industry was based on iron and coal. Today's town shows off some delightful Georgian terraces, tree-lined walkways and historic buildings which include a manor house from 1700, St Mary's church of the twisted spire and Norman tower, and The Old Lion public house (*inset*).

Apart from their entrancing names, villages around the River Rea, like Neen Savage a mile north of Cleobury and tiny Neen Sollars to the south, are delightful spots to pause. For the historian, the Roman remains of Wall Town fort are also nearby.

All the Clees and Cleoburys hereabouts are situated near the Clee range of hills, with clee and cleo probably simply being old names for 'hill'. If the history is absorbing, the present day heritage of these parts is a quite delightful find.

Shropshire, with its wonderful mix of hills, plains, valleys and meadows, is a county to explore and enjoy. It provides a rich tapestry of ancient history and modern technology, where the remains of an important 1st-century Roman city at Wroxeter, and a soaring 21st-century town, Telford, are a few miles and nearly 2,000 years apart. Through the images of expert landscape photographer Bill Meadows and the commentary of local author Shirley Tart, this book celebrates Shropshire in all its glory.

Shirley Tart lives in Coalbrookdale and is the Assistant Editor of the *Wolverhampton Express and Star*. She is also a patron of the Hope House Children's Hospice at Oswestry. During a long and eventful career she has travelled widely and covered events ranging from royal weddings to the first South African free elections. She is also the author of *Shropshire Privies*.

Bill Meadows became fascinated by landscape photography at an early age. As a teenager he experimented with an old folding camera and made countless sorties into the countryside to capture the changing face of nature within it. He is now a leading photographer whose work is increasingly requested for use in a wide variety of publications. Five volumes in this series have already been completed by Bill, including *Cheshire, Derbyshire, Leicestershire & Rutland, Warwickshire* and *Lancashire*.

Front cover photograph: The view west over Clunbury
Back cover photograph: Ironbridge